I0817281

My Little Pony

by Julie Murray

Abdo Kids Jumbo is an Imprint of Abdo Kids
abdobooks.com

abdobooks.com

Published by Abdo Kids, a division of ABDO, P.O. Box 398166, Minneapolis, Minnesota 55439.

Printed in the United States of America, North Mankato, Minnesota.

102025

012026

Photo Credits: AdobeStock, Alamy, AP Images, Everette Collection, Getty Images, REUTERS, Shutterstock, ©The Strong National Museum of Play, Rochester, New York, p.7, p13, ©Fauquier Times p.9 ©flapflapMLP p.11/CC BY-NC-SA 2.0 ©fandom p.15/CC BY-SA

Production Contributors: Teddy Borth, Jennie Forsberg, Grace Hansen
Design Contributors: Candice Keimig, Pakou Moua

Library of Congress Control Number: 2025936489

Publisher's Cataloging-in-Publication Data

Names: Murray, Julie, author.

Title: My Little Pony / by Julie Murray

Description: Minneapolis, Minnesota : Abdo Kids, 2026 | Series: Toy mania! | Includes online resources and index.

Identifiers: ISBN 9798384907572 (lib. bdg.) | ISBN 9798384908272 (ebook) | ISBN 9798384908623 (read-to-me ebook)

Subjects: LCSH: My Little Pony (Trademark)--Juvenile literature. | Toy horses--Juvenile literature. | Action figures (Toys)--Juvenile literature. | Hasbro Entertainment (Firm)--Juvenile literature. | Cartoons (Television programs)--Juvenile literature. | Toys--Juvenile literature. | Toys--History--Juvenile literature.

Classification: DDC 688.72--dc23

Table of Contents

My Little Pony 4

The Original Six 6

My Little Movies and More! 14

More Facts 22

Glossary 23

Index 24

Abdo Kids Code. 24

My Little Pony

My Little Pony rode onto the toy scene in the early 1980s. The beautiful and colorful ponies have been enjoyed by kids ever since.

My Little Pony
My Little Pony
My Little Pony
Dream Castle

The Original Six

The toy company Hasbro released the first version of My Little Pony in 1981. It was called My Pretty Pony. The toys were made of hard plastic and had **mechanical** parts. The tail and **mane** could be combed.

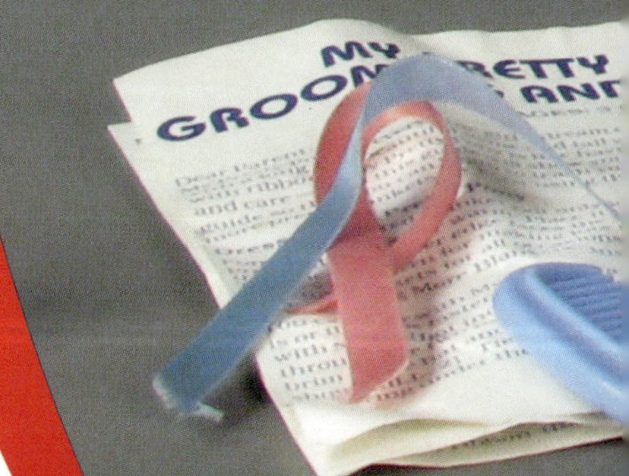

My Pretty
PONY
there) she'll wink with
one eye, wiggle her
ears . . . and even
swish her tail!
she goes to "sleep".)
© 1981 Hasbro Industries, Inc.,

The idea for My Pretty Pony came from **illustrator** Bonnie Zacherle. She worked for Hasbro. Part of her job was to come up with new toy ideas. She had always loved horses and decided to design a toy horse.

Shetland pony

Bonnie later designed a toy pony that was smaller and softer. The toy could fit in a child's hand. Hasbro released the first set in 1983. The ponies from this set are known as the Original Six.

Minty
Blossom
Snuzzle
Cotton Candy
Blue Belle
Butterscotch

The ponies came in fresh **pastel** colors. They also had “cutie marks” on their **rumps**. The line grew to include baby ponies and more. All of these became part of the first **generation** of My Little Pony toys.

Gusty
Baby Frosting
Baby Pineapple

My Little Movies and More!

My Little Pony toys were so popular that a movie was released in 1986. It was called *My Little Pony: The Movie*. The same year, a TV show called *My Little Pony 'n Friends* was created.

My Little Pony
The Movie
My Little Pony
'n Friends

In 2010, the television series *My Little Pony: Friendship is Magic* hit screens. The main characters taught viewers about friendship and kindness. There are My Little Pony toys based on characters from the show.

The shows and movies introduced each pony's magical powers. Twilight Sparkle can create magic potions. Rainbow Dash can control the weather.

Today, the magic of My Little Pony is enjoyed by all ages! Some fans meet up dressed as their favorite characters. There are even clothing lines **inspired** by My Little Pony.

More Facts

- The Original Six ponies are named Blossom, Blue Belle, Butterscotch, Cotton Candy, Minty, and Snuzzle.
- My Little Ponies live in a town called Ponyville in the kingdom of Equestria.
- My Little Pony was **inducted** into the National Toy Hall of Fame in 2024.

Glossary

generation – a group of things that are released at the same time.

illustrator – an artist who draws or creates pictures.

inducted – brought in as a member.

inspired – given a new idea by something.

mane – the long hair on the head and neck of horses.

mechanical – made of or having to do with machines.

pastel – a pale, soft color.

rump – the back section of an animal's body.

Index

characters 18

colors 12

Hasbro 6, 8, 10

markings 12

My Little Pony: Friendship Is Magic 16

My Little Pony: The Movie 14

My Little Pony 'n Friends 14

Original Six, the 10

Zacherle, Bonnie 8, 10